Embroidery : new approaches

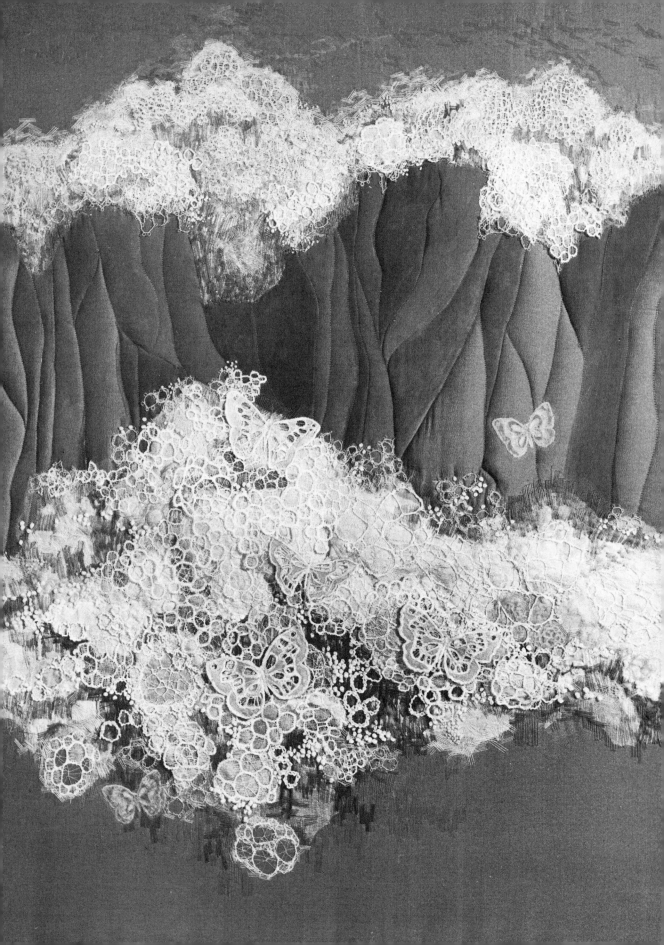

Embroidery:
new approaches

Jan Beaney

Photographs by Dudley Moss

PELHAM BOOKS

First published in Great Britain by
Pelham Books Ltd
52 Bedford Square
London WC1B 3EF
1978

ISBN 0 7207 1072 3

Printed in Great Britain by
BAS Printers Limited, Over Wallop, Hampshire

Frontispiece
A Secret Place: machine quilted shapes applied to a rayon ground
fabric, some of the shapes were painted with Dylon fabric paint.
Machined cut work flowers and butterflies were worked on muslin,
scrim, bleached vegetable bags. The knots and straight stitches were
worked in a variety of fine wools and cotton threads.

For my parents

Acknowledgements

I would like to thank the following people for their enthusiasm, help and encouragement in the preparation of this book: Alan Wysman, Roger Cuthbert, Denys Short and Lawrence Cresswell for supplying additional photographs; Audrey Brockbank, Julia Caprara, Eirian Short, Audrey Tucker, Audrey Walker, Richard Box, Jane Clarke, Beryl Court, Penny Cuthbert, Catherine Dowden, Jean Littlejohn, Bryony Neilson, and Beverley Nixon for allowing me to use photographs of their work; and Pam Dennett for typing the script.

My very special thanks to Dudley Moss for his splendid photographs, to Lynn Moss for correcting my text, to Jane Clarke and Audrey Walker for their constant encouragement and to my husband Steve, who was always willing to help throughout the preparation of this book.

All photographs are by Dudley Moss unless otherwise credited.

All drawings and embroideries are by the author unless otherwise credited.

Contents

Introduction

This book is for the many people who are excited by the medium of modern embroidery and who want to create their own designs with fabrics and threads—but are not sure how to start. Some are confident about making designs and working in colour, but lack experience of working in this particular medium. Others, having worked with materials, are apprehensive about drawing and design. It is hoped that this book will teach the necessary skills and help the beginner to gain confidence and enjoyment from designing and creating original work.

The subject of embroidery is so extensive that only one main area—designing and working pictures or panels—is considered in this book. However, many of the methods of working and especially approaches to design, colour and texture will be helpful for anyone wishing to work household, dress or church embroidery. (Although with these latter types of embroidery there are other considerations to bear in mind: whether the article is to be washed, ironed or worn and whether the colour, design or fabric is suitable for its function.)

As well as building up a knowledge of various stitches, methods of embroidery and an awareness of colour, texture and sources of design, the reader will be helped to criticize her own work. With experience she will be able to proceed to the next stage of her development on her own. Guide lines and suggestions on ways to develop designs are given but not the complete solution, so that the individual creativity of the artist remains.

To avoid confusion while the beginner is gaining experience, the choices of approach to the varying stages of embroidery have been limited to those that I have found most helpful for students in my own teaching work. To balance this, in the

Water Garden—detail. Hessian ground. Applied fabrics include velvet, hessian, leather, silk, rayon and gold P.V.C. Wool and cotton threads were used for couching, french knots and straight stitches; looped tape, padded areas and beads were also used.

8

concluding section, I have tried to indicate the great variety of approaches of experienced artists by including examples of professional embroiderers, together with their own comments on their work.

After reading this book, you should be able to make your own designs. But the stages introduced here are only the initial steps in discovering this vast and varied subject. Visit textile exhibitions, read books on allied subjects, experiment with stitchery and, most important of all, continue to look and draw so that you gather a number of ideas to interpret in fabric and thread.

Detail of *Garden Patchwork* by Audrey Walker. See page 30.

Stages in developing an embroidered panel

Although some experienced embroiderers work directly and intuitively on fabrics, it is suggested that, initially, the following basic plan of action is used.

1   Make a design.
2   Square up the design to the required size.
3   Choose colour scheme.
4   Select background fabric.
5   Take a tracing of the design—basic shapes only.
6   Cut up the tracing to make a paper pattern.
7   Choose materials to apply.
8   Using the paper patterns, cut out the material shapes and pin to background fabric, taking care to place correctly. (Refer to original design.)
9   Consider carefully whether it is suitable or beneficial to develop parts of the design with other fabrics such as nets, scrims, knitted or padded shapes.
10 Sew fabrics in place.
11 Select a variety of threads in the chosen colour scheme.
12 Build up the *whole* design initially with line stitches or blocks of stitches to emphasize basic shapes, focal point, movement, etc. (Do not get involved with small areas and details at this stage.)
13 Finally, work textured stitches and smaller details.
14 Stretch if necessary.
15 Mount and frame.

The following set of photographs has been included to show *one way* a design can be developed from the paper design to a finished piece of work. It is not intended for the reader to copy, although a similar exercise could be attempted, but to help anyone who has not worked in the medium before to have a clearer idea of the various stages in making an embroidered panel. It should also be a useful reference and background structure for the following sections.

Drawing: tree roots (ink/wash).

Above right
Cut-paper pattern inspired by drawing of tree roots.

Right
The design was transferred by placing the cut-paper pattern on to the ground fabric and tacking round the edges.

12

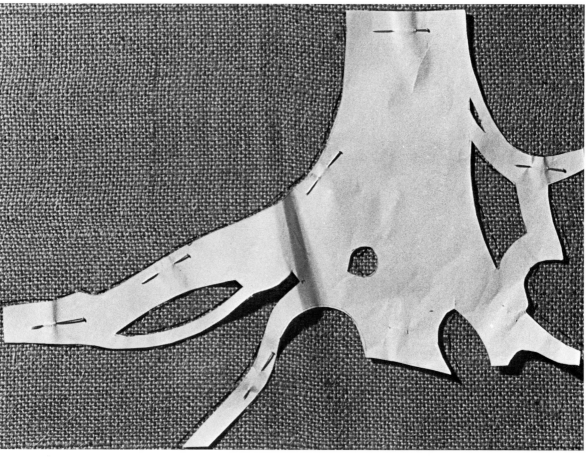

Two layers of net were cut
slightly larger than the basic
shape. One was placed on the
ground fabric. The paper pattern
was used again to cut out a shape
in a scrim cloth. This was then
placed on top of the net and the
second layer of net placed on top
of the scrim. Small pieces of net
were also applied to darken the
cavity areas. The net was stitched
in place with a fine matching
coloured thread just inside the
edges of the shapes.

At this stage some of the top
layer of net was cut away to
expose the scrim cloth. The net
was left covering the edges of the
cloth to prevent further fraying.
Strips of scrim were applied with
the edges turned under and slip-
stitched in place. Patches padded
with felt were also added.

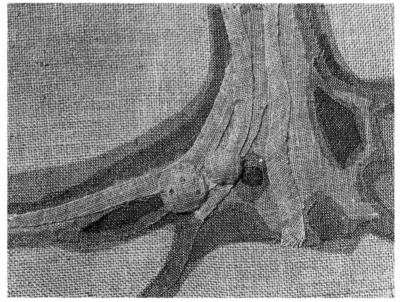

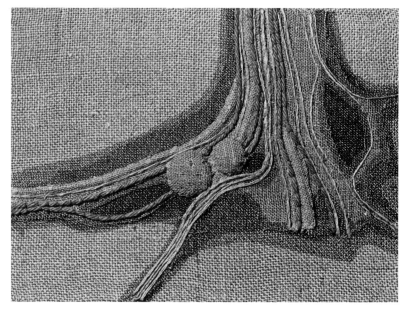

Threads pulled from hessian and cotton threads were couched to re-define the design. The applied areas were slightly padded by inserting thick threads.

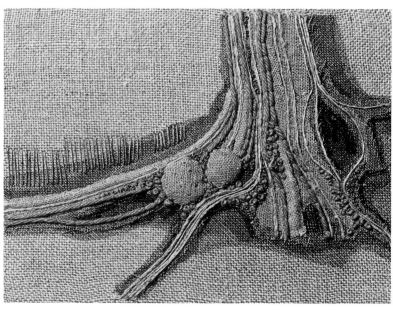

Straight stitches in a darker thread were used to emphasize the shadows. Knots worked in wool and cotton perle threads were used to build up areas of texture.

Materials to collect for designing

1   Sketches, photographs, books—sources of design
2   Plain white paper
3   Coloured papers—sugar, pastel, tissue, paper torn from magazines
4   Tracing paper
5   Pencils (HB, 2B) felt pens, crayons
6   Paint brush—and paints, ink, dyes
7   Cow gum / P.V.A. (Marvin medium)
8   Masking tape
9   Scissors

Below left
Drawing of patterns on a stone (ink/wash).

Below right
Drawing of sweets (including nougat, almond flakes, English mixture, beach balls, rock fruits).

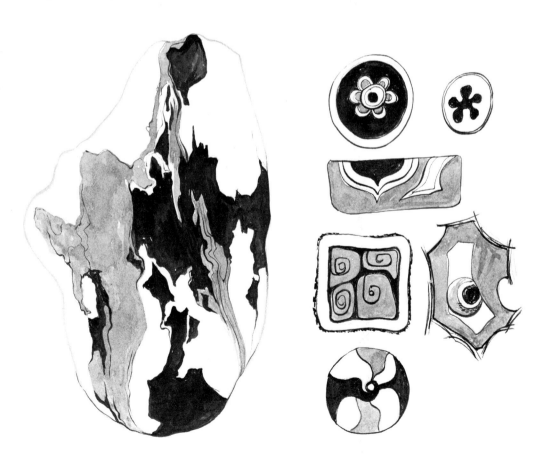

Sources of design

If you are new to the medium and to designing, do not choose vast, complicated subjects. Work through the following suggestions and when you have gained confidence in your ability to design and create patterns, only then extend your range of working.

In the first instance, learn to *look closely at everyday things*. Organize your looking into certain areas as suggested below.

Look for patterns

1   in gardens (shapes of leaves, flower petals, alpine plants)
2   in hedgerows (wild flowers, grasses, hedges)
3   on rocks (pebbles, shells, seaweed)
4   on buildings (decorative brickwork, wood and stone carving, doors, windows)
5   on machinery (cogs, wheels, chains, levers)
6   in the countryside ('patchwork' fields, tree roots, fungus)
7   in the kitchen (cross-sections of cabbage, cucumber, tomato, pepper, melon, sweets, cakes, open sandwiches)
8   in museums (patterns from jewelry, textiles, pottery, armour, furniture, minerals and other natural forms)

Drawing: pattern from polished agate.

Textures

1   Look at and touch different surfaces.
2   Take prints and rubbings: they often reveal more patterns than the eye is first aware of.
3   Be sensitive to differences in surfaces—tree bark, the skin of a peach, cat's fur, shingle on a beach, etc.

17

Follow your looking by drawing. Initially choose small subjects—a porchway, window or one flower—so that you have fewer drawing problems. Take care to draw the main shapes first, followed by the less important ones, leaving the finer details until last. Consider the background spaces between the shapes as your drawing progresses. In time, draw more complicated subjects such as foam, washing-up bubbles, water patterns, clouds or tiny patterns taken from stones, shells or insects when seen under a magnifying glass. After drawing small subjects and training your eye to appreciate proportions and background shapes, you will be able to tackle bigger subjects such as trees, landscapes, figures, buildings.

Practising simple exercises is essential when learning to play a musical instrument: the same rule applies to drawing, too.

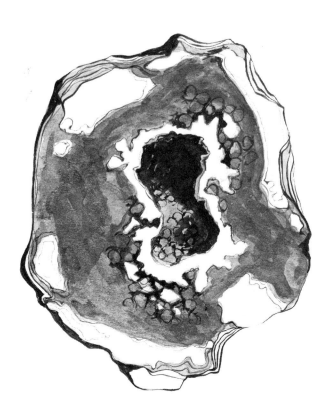

Drawing of a cross-section of a flintstone (ink/wash).

Opposite
Decorative stone archways (Saxon). Christchurch, Dorset.

18

Until you have built up a collection of reference drawings and photographs, choose simple motifs for your embroidery: for example, expanded paper shapes (see page 21), motifs inspired by designs in museums, or any of the patterns suggested on page 17.

Subjects such as butterflies, fish and birds can be a good source of design. Take drawings or photographs from life or by visiting museums, zoos, or by referring to books. Do not copy exactly or try to improve their natural beauty, but select areas you particularly like. Simplify or exaggerate certain aspects. Enlarge and emphasize some patterns, simplify or disregard others. If you wish to make a more stylized design, make some of the outlines bolder, more geometric or fluid, whichever the initial pattern suggests to you. For instance, some markings on a butterfly's wing are very complicated. Select a small area only and enlarge it to fit the wing shape. Another approach would be to choose only a small part of the wing to work, leaving the remaining shapes as a plainer, less defined pattern.

Romano-British brooch (ink).
British Museum.

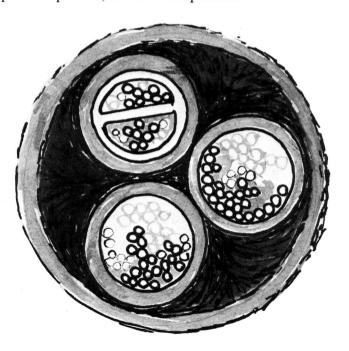

Drawing (cross section) of
electric cables (Science Museum).

Having found a motif, it is often helpful to forget its original identity and embroider it in materials and threads in any colour you wish, emphasizing any parts that particularly excite you. Experiment by working the background shapes and not the basic design, or embroider the main shapes leaving the outline suggested but unworked.

Cut-paper designs

After making a linear design, it is often a good idea to build up the same design in paper. This has the advantage of making you see the picture in simple basic shapes. You can develop the whole design and not be sidetracked by surface details.

You can also design directly with paper:

1   Cut various shapes which are sympathetic to each other:
(*a*) different-sized circles
(*b*) thick, thin, long and short curving lines
(*c*) rectangles, squares, lines, stripes.

Make a pattern by placing the paper pieces on another sheet of paper, preferably of a contrasting colour, making sure the background spaces are pleasing and not so big that the paper shapes become isolated from each other and spoil the unity of design.

2   Expanding shapes:

Cut a circle, square or rectangle of paper into pieces, contrasting large and small shapes. On another sheet of paper re-assemble them in their initial positions allowing background spaces to show between.

Toadstool—embroidery. Applied fabrics include leather, satin, and ruched rayon with couched threads, whipped cords and straight stitches (Jean Littlejohn).

Toadstool (ink) by Jean Littlejohn.

Simplified drawing to enable a paper pattern to be made.

Plants by the water's edge.

A design inspired by the photograph above. Some leaf and background shapes have been emphasized, others have been omitted.

Opposite
Drawing of a passion flower in bud (*a*), with areas of the drawing (*b, c, d*) taken out of context with certain parts of the plant or background shapes emphasized.

Trees as a source of design. The drawings show two approaches: one emphasizes and simplifies the main shapes and spaces between, the other shows the textured qualities.

Right
Old gnarled tree (ink).

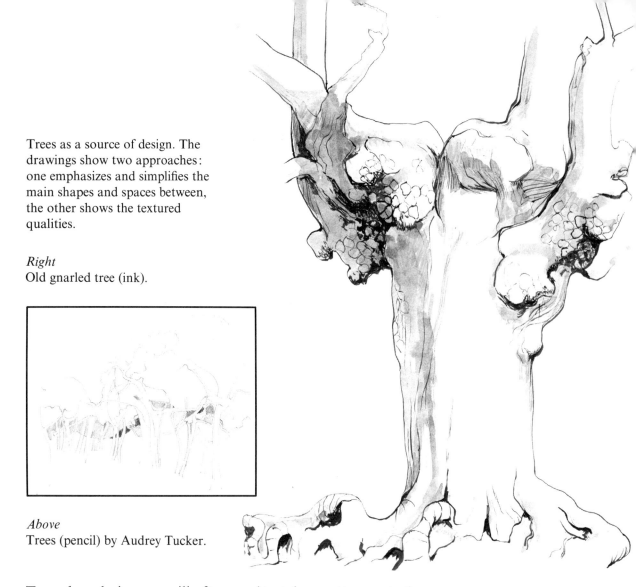

Above
Trees (pencil) by Audrey Tucker.

To make a design you will often need to take a pattern out of context. Cut small paper frames in varying sizes, place on a drawing, photograph, rubbing or print and select an area you like. Take care to note if there will be a centre of interest, that all shapes are pleasing to the eye and, most important of all, that the selected area retains the characteristics that first attracted you to the subject.

When you feel more familiar with the medium, be more adventurous with your designs. Instead of placing a simple motif in space, compose a design where some shapes or lines meet the outside edges of the panel. Textured rubbings and prints, bark, flower beds, landscape and machinery are all possible starting points for this type of composition.

26

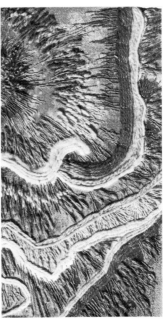

A photograph of a toadstool with an area selected. (Photo Roger Cuthbert, L.R.P.S.)

An embroidery inspired by the photograph above. Cotton ground, cretan stitch, knots and couching worked in a variety of cotton threads (Jean Littlejohn).

Sedum—a selected area as a
possible design source.

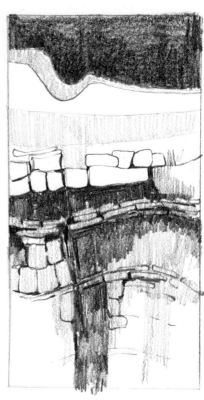

A section selected from the
drawing below to work as a design.

Sketch of a quarry (ink/wash).

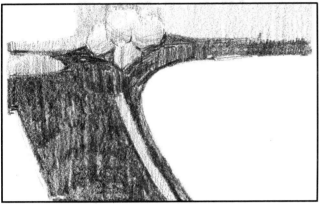

Four sketches of the same view slightly altering the position of the group of trees, the chosen focal point. Always experiment with your composition so that the focal point and surrounding shapes are pleasing to your eye.

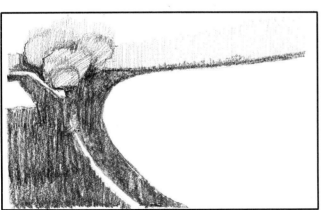

29

Garden patchwork by Audrey Walker. Patchwork ground. Applied fabrics include lace, nets and rayons. Stitches include cretan, knots and straight stitches. This is a very good example of the focal point being emphasized by a gradual build-up of tones and textural interest. (Photo Lawrence Cresswell.)

Points to remember when making a design

1 Contrast (*a*) large and small shapes

             (*b*) 'busy' sections of detail, texture or movement with plainer quieter ones

             (*c*) line and mass

             (*d*) dark and light tones.

2 Exaggerate or simplify certain parts.

3 Develop and be aware of background spaces.

4 Select a part of your panel to be a focal point.

5 Place shapes and lines carefully to 'lead the eye' into or around focal point.

6 Take care when positioning dark, light or brightly coloured shapes. They could distract attention from the focal point.

Colour

Exciting discoveries can be made experimenting with colour harmonies, complimentary and discordant colour factors. But this is a vast subject with too many aspects to cover fully here, and anyone wishing to extend their knowledge of the subject should consult some of the books listed on page 95.

For the embroiderer, finding new colour schemes is of prime importance. Initially, you must learn to look closely at everything around you to discover colour. You can find unusual colour schemes from materials stacked in builders' yards, the old brick and slate of a Victorian house, the sun glistening on a rain drop, a tropical fish, a feather—the list is endless.

Be aware of the colour changes during each season of the year. The weather or time of day can also change the emphasis of colour. For example, the sea is one colour on a sunny day and another on a grey, stormy one. Be adventurous and avoid the old colour combinations so often displayed in shop windows. Note down possible colour schemes so that you can use the reference later to influence any embroidery you wish to work.

You may find the following suggestions helpful:

Opposite
White Tree by Jan Beaney. Hessian ground with applied hessian, satin, scrim, domette and net. Threads include cord, knitting wools, carpet thrums, embroidery cottons, macramé and weaving yarns worked in couching, straight stitches and french knots.

1   Working in one colour with varying tones:
Roses, cornflowers, hebe at varying stages: one shade in the bud, another in full flower and a paler tone when dying.
Cross-sections of cabbage, lettuce or tomato.
Sunflowers—petals in full sunlight—others in the shade.
Euphorbia flowers (in Spring)—all tones of green.

Summer Window I by Audrey
Walker. Applied fabrics include
laces, nets and chiffons. Machine
embroidery and some hand
stitching.

Summer Window I—detail.

Astrentia.

2   Working in colour 'families':
   Nasturtiums—all tones of red, yellow and orange.
   Lichen—orange, brown, ginger, cinnamon.

3   Working with a main colour scheme plus small areas of
other colour:
   Varying greens (as seen in a hedgerow) with white
   (daisies) or purple (vetch).
   Astrentia—varying greens, white with a touch of cerise
   pink.
   Euphorbia flowers (faded)—varying greens with
   patches of rust or deep red.
   Honesty seedheads (before they turn silver)—shades of
   maroon, purple, brown with areas of yellow/green.
   Tiny sections of colour taken from shells or pebbles or
   stones. You may find an unusual scheme such as one
   with shades of apricot, orange and beige contrasted by
   tiny areas of navy blue and grey.

Background materials

Many materials are suitable for use as a background, including hessian, linen scrim, and even-weave curtain fabrics made of synthetics such as polyester and acrylic. But choose a fairly firm, strong material if you intend applying lots of fabrics and stitchery.

Choose a 'good tempered' fabric such as hessian for your first pieces of work. It is cheaper than most curtain fabrics of the same weight, is made in a splendid range of colours and is easy to work on. In some instances, hessian might be too heavy a background for more delicate work, and linen scrim or 'linen look' dress fabrics would be more suitable.

If a tightly woven rayon or silk is used, take care not to tear through the fabric when working a heavier thread. Make a hole in the cloth with a stiletto to enable you to pull needle and thread through more easily and choose stitches that are worked mainly on the top of the material.

Left: cotton scrim.
Right: hessian.

These fabrics can be bought from specialist suppliers, and the soft-furnishing and 'art needlework' sections of most department stores.

Points to remember:

In general

1 Do not choose loosely woven fabrics as they will pull out of shape when lots of fabric and thread are applied to them.

2 Avoid ridged or very tightly woven cloth, such as repp, as stitching can be very difficult.

3 A heavily textured or brightly coloured thread woven into the material might be too noticeable and detract from the design you intend working.

4 The same consideration applies to boldly woven or printed patterned fabrics unless it is an essential part of the design and has been considered from the start.

Threads–and needles

Threads

Collect all types of threads—thick, thin, matt, shiny, rough and smooth. Sort and store them in colour 'families' for easier use.

Experiment by stitching with the most unusual or unlikely threads to find their range of applications. Textured knitting and weaving yarns are best when couched or worked over existing threads; their slubs and loops make it difficult to pull them through fabrics, and they easily break. Smoother linen, cotton and wool threads are more suitable for intricate stitchery.

A variety of threads which include knitting wools, macramé and weaving yarns, chenille, wool carpet thrums, lurex and cotton crochet yarns, cotton, rayon and woollen embroidery threads.

Some special weaving yarns, carpet thrums and embroidery threads such as perle, chenille, linen and gold threads can only be obtained from specialist shops. However, a reasonable range of embroidery cottons, wools and many novelty knitting, crochet and macramé threads can be found in department stores and handicraft shops.

Needles

Collect an assortment of needles; the following are particularly useful:

Bead needles—for bead embroidery.

Needles with large eyes, e.g. knitter's needles, large embroidery needles, short-pile rug needles—for work with thick threads.

A stiletto is also a useful tool for making holes in fabric when stitching with thicker threads or fabric strips.

Frames

It is not necessary to have a frame to make an embroidered panel, but many stitches and techniques are more effective and easier to work when the background fabric is tautly stretched. However, some embroiderers prefer to work some stitches without a frame and this you can only learn by experience.

The method of stretching the background fabric over a frame is quite simple. Having tacked or drawn the design on first and, in some instances, applied the fabrics, also, stretch the material over a suitably sized frame taking care to keep the warp and weft at right-angles to the edges of the frame. Use a staple gun or drawing pins to fix in place. Some designers stretch the fabric on the frame for the initial stages of building up the design, temporarily remove the panel to apply the fabrics by machine, and then re-stretch to complete the work.

Any of the following can be used as a frame:

Old picture frames—from jumble sales, junk shops and auctions.
Canvas stretchers—from artist's material suppliers. Buy in separate lengths and make up to required size.
Slate frame—from Embroidery specialists, Art needlework departments.
Home-made frames.

Frames: Canvas stretcher (*outer*)
Home-made frame (*inner*).

Squaring up designs

Having decided on the required size of design, choose a larger sheet of paper with the same proportions as the original design. Fold into sections or draw carefully measured lines on the original design and the larger sheet of paper as illustrated. On the new paper, copy the design from the original, each corresponding section at a time. Indicate outlines first, follow with the details. With care, each section should match up to make the scaled-up whole. If the design is very complicated, divide the paper into smaller sections.

Scaling up (squaring up) your design from the original plan.

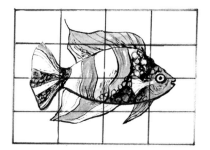

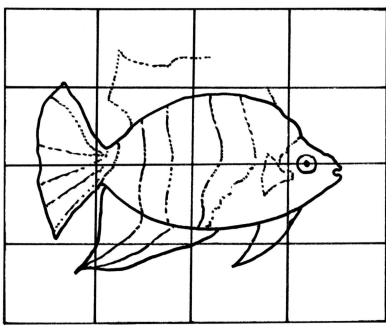

Transferring the design

There are many ways of transferring the design on to the background material. The three methods given opposite will be the most helpful:

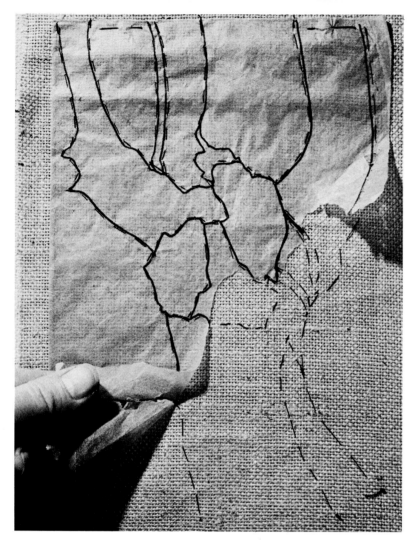

Transferring the design: trace the design on to tissue paper. Pin or tack on to the ground fabric. With a fine thread, tack through the tissue paper and fabric taking care to follow the designs carefully. Fasten and finish off the thread securely. Tear away the paper to expose the tacked design.

1   Take a tracing of your design (basic shapes only). Cut out the main shapes and re-assemble on the background material making sure that they are in the correct position. Having built up the whole design, pin the paper pieces in place and tack or chalk round the shapes. (See page 13.)

2   Trace the design on to thin paper and pin this on to the background fabric. Tack through the paper drawing, following the lines accurately, and taking care to fasten the thread on and off securely. Tear away the paper to reveal the tacked design.

3   Draw freely on to the background material with french chalk or a white pencil. Tack over lines when you are satisfied with the design.

41

Appliqué

As a general rule, the fabric shapes to be applied should be cut so that, when they are sewn in place, the warp and weft threads match those of the background fabric. This will reduce puckering. However, this rule can be broken if the design requires certain effects. Frayed edges could be applied in various directions or shot fabrics placed with the threads at differing angles so that the tones and colours change with the angle of the light on them.

Collect as many varied fabrics as you can. Coarse linens, knobbly tweed, fine muslin, rough hessian, leather, silks, and rayons are only a few from a vast range of materials that you could acquire as scraps or remnants from dressmaking friends, markets and material shops.

Be adventurous when applying fabrics. Some of the following suggestions might be suitable for building up a rich surface before stitching begins:

1   Contrast matt and shiny, smooth and rough surfaces.
2   Build up some areas with layers of net, scrim or tarlatan.
3   Cut away parts to expose materials beneath.
4   Apply loosely woven fabrics, possibly pulling out some threads or rearranging the order of the threads into holes of various sizes and shapes.

Methods of applying fabric to the background material

1 Fabrics which fray can be applied by:

    (a) herringbone stitch
    (b) using zig-zag stitch on a sewing machine
    (c) turning edges under and slip-stitching
    (d) backing with iron-on vilene and slip-stitching (but not all fabrics are suitable)

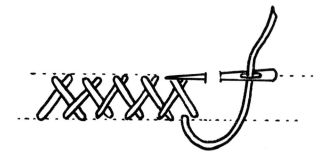

Herringbone stitch.

Appliqué sample showing
(*a*) fabric sewn down by
herringbone stitch;
(*b*) leather, felt slipstitched;
(*c*) net sewn down with tiny
stitches;
(*d*) fabric backed with iron-on
vilene and slipstitched.

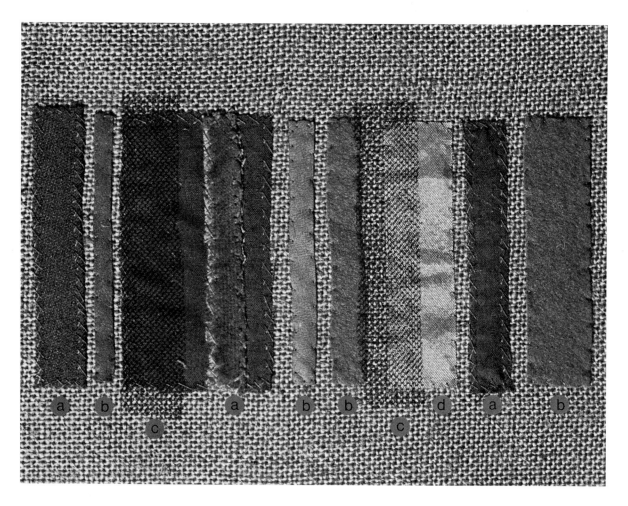

White Tree—detail. Applied satin, net, scrim on a hessian ground. Small areas of domette and net have been cut or pulled into holes to show the fabric beneath.

2 Non-fraying fabrics such as leather and felt need only be slip-stitched in place.

3 Net can be applied by little 'catch' stitches near the outside edges.

In general, use a fine thread in a colour to match the material. All stitches should be done in an unobtrusive way so as not to compete with any surface stitching to follow.

Textures

The designs in this section have been included in the hope that they will suggest ideas for further work in creating new and interesting textural surfaces. Everyone sees different qualities in everyday scenes and objects and will therefore exaggerate or eliminate different aspects. Therefore, interpretations of various surfaces must be very personal and the following suggestions are only included to provide possible starting points.

Shot silk, fine chiffons, muslin, net and other transparent materials might suggest flowers, skin, sky or insects' wings. Ruched, tufted, knotted and looped surfaces could be a way of interpreting flower gardens, hedgerows and fields. Rock formations or gnarled tree roots could be built up with padded, rolled, tucked and knitted patches. Stitches deliberately worked in layers in a haphazard way might suggest leaves and undergrowth while beads, shisha glass, silver thread or lacy stitchery might be useful to show swirling water, foam, blossom or snowy scenes.

Keep all experiments as they may well suggest certain effects to use in future embroideries.

Trapunto or stuffed quilting: tack together the top fabric and a backing material such as scrim, muslin or other lightweight fabric.
(a) front of work: machine or backstitch the shape to be padded through both layers of fabric.
(b) back of work: cut or carefully pull aside the threads of the lining fabric only. Take care not to cut the top fabric. Insert wadding evenly to the required shape. (Use Acrylic waste or similar material available from department stores or handicraft shops. If using cotton wool, make sure it is shredded or teased out, or the padding will be lumpy.)
(c) back of work: oversew or herringbone the edges of the cut fabric to complete.

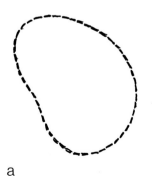

a

b

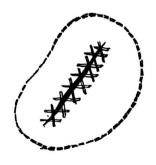

c

Experimental embroidery:
hessian ground with ruched satin,
scrim, lurex rayon, and padded
satin patches applied. Stitches
include couched cord and french
knots worked in various wools,
perle and perlita threads. China
and glass beads sewn down with
Perivale silk.

Opposite
Snow at Easter by Audrey
Walker. One side of a three-
dimensional structure. On a
calico ground fabric, stylized tree
shapes have been worked with
trapunto padding (see diagram
p. 45), couched threads, and
backstitch. Knitted pieces have
been applied to the foreground.

46

When working on a panel, always ask yourself if the
particular action you are about to take will enhance or
enrich it. So often textures are used because the designer
likes the effect without giving due consideration to whether
it suits the particular panel being worked. Experiment,
discover, invent—but be discerning.

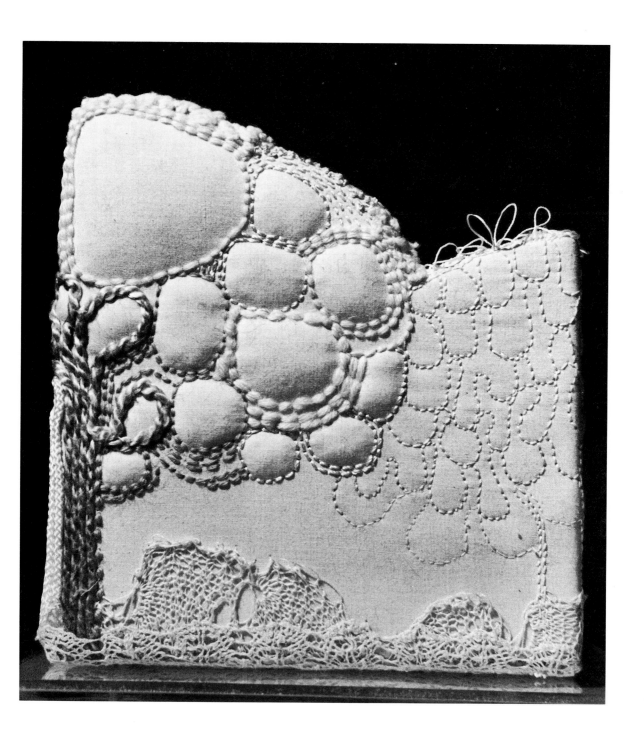

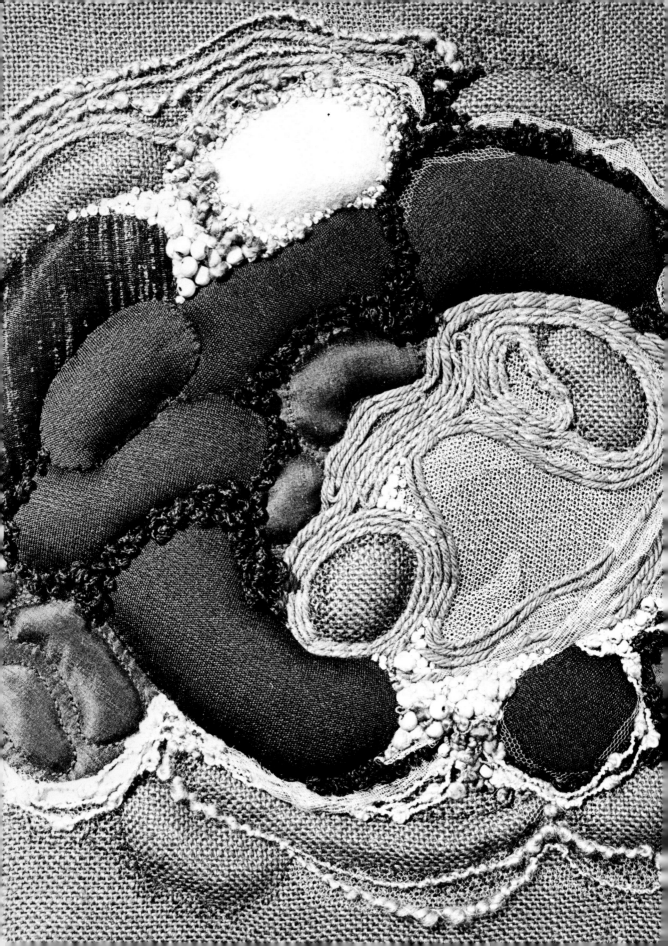

Opposite
Design (by Beryl Court) incorporating applied padded patches, trapunto padding with applied fabrics, trapunto using the ground fabric with a backing fabric applied beneath (see diagram p. 45). Stitches include couching, looped threads, knots and bead work.

Rhododendron Tunnel by Jan Beaney. Hessian ground, applied rayons, satin, nets. Ruched and looped fabrics and threads. Couching, knots and straight stitches worked in tape, knitting, weaving and embroidery cotton and wools.

Detail from *Watergarden* by Jan Beaney. Leather and velvet leaves applied to padded areas. P.V.C., looped tape, knots and beads provide other textural interest.

Detail from a panel by Audrey
Walker. Wool and cotton
embroidery threads worked in
cretan stitch, french knots,
seeding, and one-sided raised
chain band.

Poppies and Nasturtiums by
Audrey Tucker.

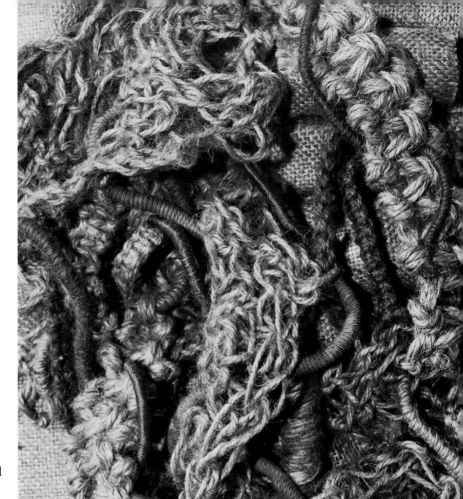

Right
Detail from an experimental panel: hessian ground. Applied knitted strips, whipped and macramé cords: some worked in jute string, others in soft embroidery and perle cottons (Jane Clarke).

Below
Detail from an experimental panel: hessian ground. Applied whipped and finger cords, knitted strips, net bags, nylon tights and wooden beads (Beryl Court).

Golden Pond—detail. Padded
areas built up in a strong cotton
fabric. Leaves worked in velvet,
leather and other vilene-backed
fabrics. Gold P.V.C. was used for
the water area. Threads include
macramé cord, wools, perle and
sewing cottons. Weaving yarns,
scrim, and glass beads were also
used.

Opposite
Straight stitches worked in strips
of silk and rayon, knitting wools
and tape.

51

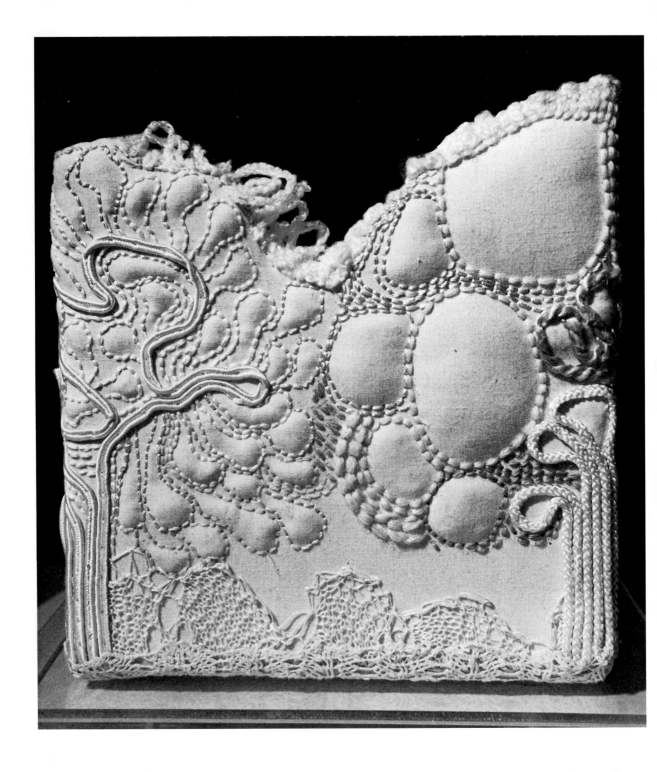

Snow at Easter. Audrey Walker.
Stylized tree designs showing
couched cords.

Stitches

Couching

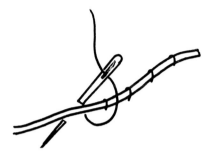

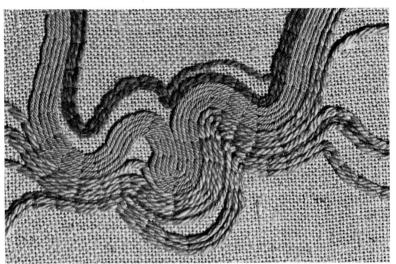

Thicker thread sewn down with a finer thread in a matching colour. The ends of the thicker yarn should be taken through to the back of the fabric and fastened down with the fine thread.

Above right
Sample includes couched wool, macramé cord and candlewick cotton.

Detail from an experimental panel (Beryl Court). Hessian ground, couched cords, plastic strips (vegetable bags) dishcloth and nylon tights. Knitted areas worked in wool and 'vest' cotton.

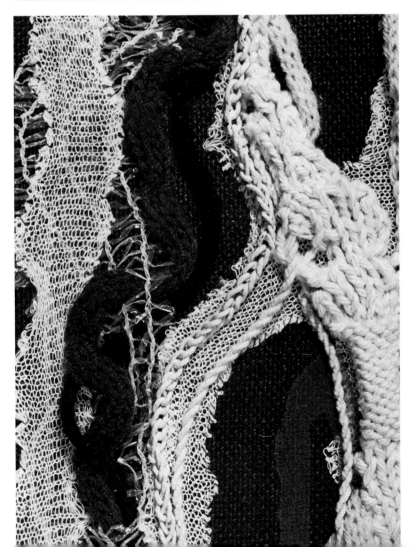

Double knot stitch

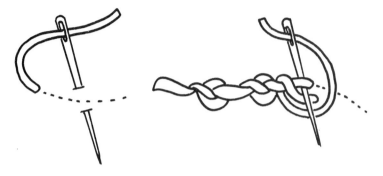

Double knot stitch.

Stitches worked in various wools, shiny macramé, tubular rayon cord and perle cotton.

Chain stitch

Threads include wool, tubular rayon cord, and plastraw. Worked in wool, string, perle, perlita, and soft embroidery cotton.

Twisted chain

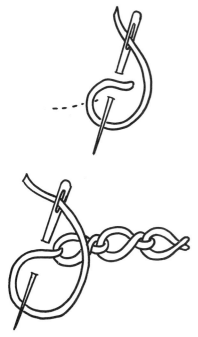

Twisted chain stitch.

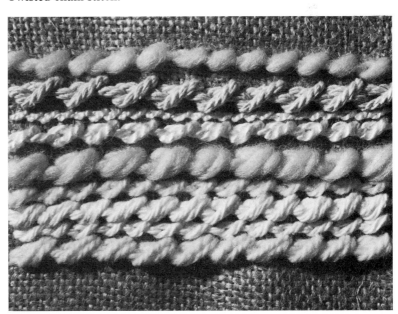

Raised chain band

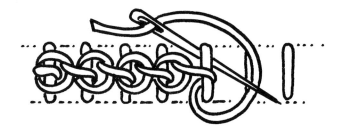

Below
Raised chain band. Work the
base ladder stitches first and
follow with the surface stitchery.

Left
Design inspired by bark rubbings
(Penny Cuthbert). Most areas
worked in raised chain band in
varying threads with french
knots.

Opposite
Worked in double strands of
macramé cord and wool carpet
thrums. The sample shows the
stitch worked in several layers to
give a chunky effect.

Backstitch wheel

Back stitch wheels: work eight stitches into the centre; bring the thread out near the centre and work over and under the stitch behind and/or under the next stitch. Repeat this action all the way round until the desired effect is obtained.

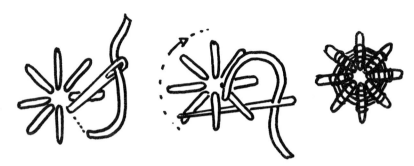

Back stitch wheels (Jane Clarke). Sample shows the stitches worked in wool, cotton perle and soft embroidery cotton.

Opposite
Experimental stitchery (Beryl Court). Areas of raised chain band worked in cotton yarn in several directions and built up in layers on some parts. Wooden beads were added to enrich some of the cavities.

Knotted cable chain

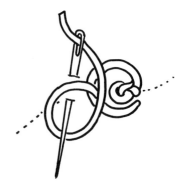

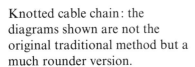

Knotted cable chain: the
diagrams shown are not the
original traditional method but a
much rounder version.

Knotted cable chain worked in
embroidery wools and cottons.

Opposite
Sampler showing mostly knotted
cable chain with raised chain
band, bullion and french knots in
wools and cottons (Catherine
Dowden).

Fly stitch

Fly stitch worked in: wool and perle cotton (*above right*); and matt, shiny, thick and thin cottons and wools by Beverley Nixon (*below right*).

Opposite (above)
wools, macramé cord, candlewick and perle.

Opposite (below)
Fly stitch worked in a variety of directions mainly in matt carpet thrums with small areas of shiny perle cotton (Beryl Court).

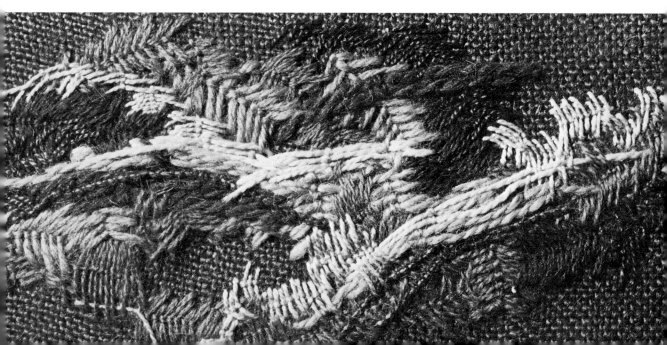

Pulled holes

Pulled holes: loosely woven
curtain fabric pulled into holes
and stitched with matt wool and
shiny cotton threads.

Red Love Fall by Julia Caprara.
Pulled holes, knots, loops and
tassels worked in a variety of
wools, chenille and embroidery
cotton. Fabric strips and beads
were also used.

Rain Palace by Julia Caprara.
Scrim ground pulled into holes;
straight stitches, eyelet holes,
tassels and knots worked in fine
wools and fabric strips.

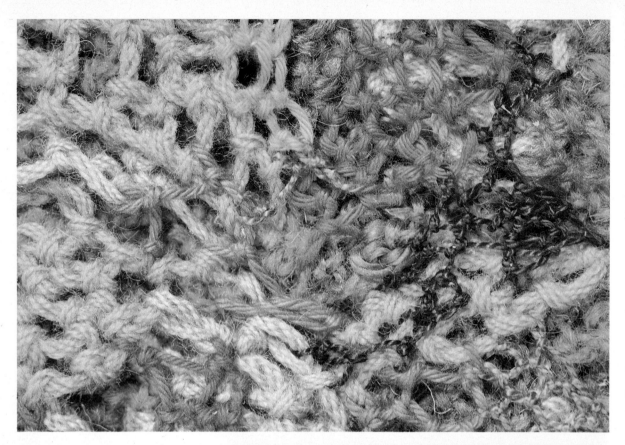

Experimental stitches by Bryony
Neilson. Knotted buttonhole
filling stitch worked in varying
directions and layers in matt
and shiny cotton and wool
threads.

Detail of panel showing needle-
weaving, buttonhole, loops
and fringing in fine wool,
stranded and twisted cotton
threads (Audrey Walker).

Wave stitch

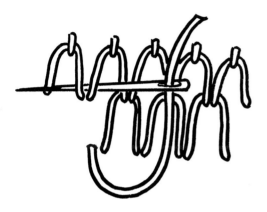

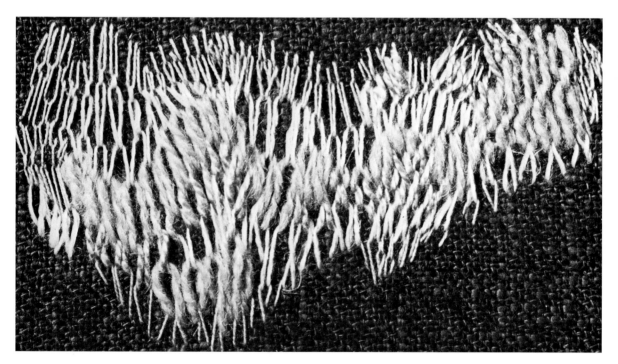

First work vertical straight
stitches. Hessian ground, wave
stitch worked in thick and thin
threads, carpet wool, cotton perle
and linen thread (Diana
Dalmahoy).

Feather stitch

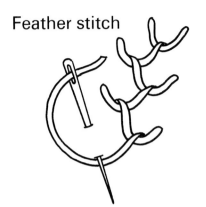

Spanish knotted feather

Sample of Spanish knotted
feather worked in wool, cotton
perle and one strand of stranded
cotton (Jane Clarke).

Cretan stitch

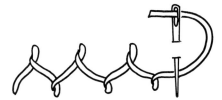

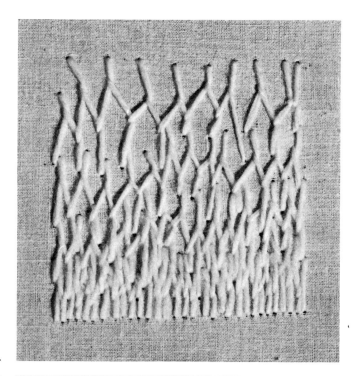

Cretan stitch.

Above
Blocks of cretan stitch worked in varying knitting wools, strips of chiffon, macramé tubular rayon cord and raffene.

Right
Cretan stitch worked in several threads and varying spacing giving subtle tonal changes.

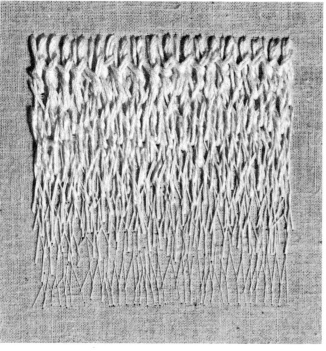

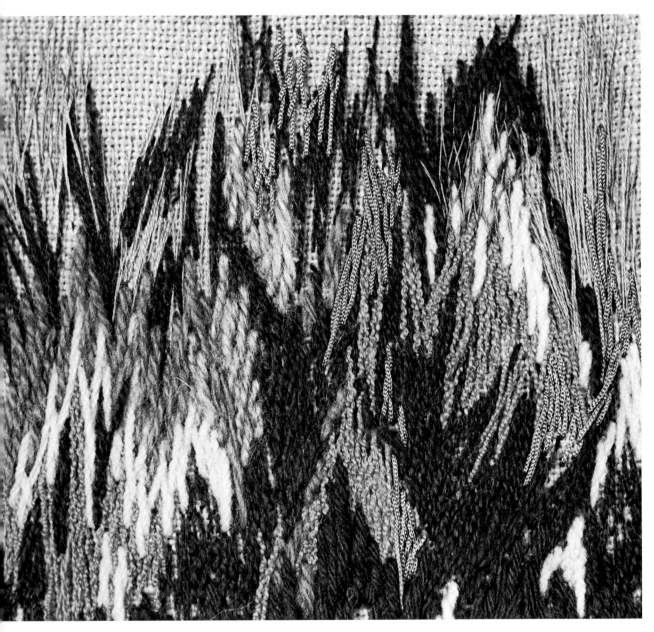

Above
Cretan stitches in long spiky
stitches worked in various wools,
knitting yarns, tubular rayon
cord and cotton embroidery
threads (Jean Littlejohn).

Right
Cretan stitch worked in wools,
candlewick cotton, crochet, perle
and stranded cottons.

French knots

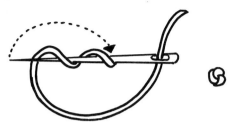

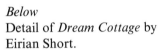

Right
Sample shows various sized knots worked in double and single strands of knitting wool, plastraw, perle cotton.

Below
Detail of *Dream Cottage* by Eirian Short.

Detail of centre of *Rhododendron Tunnel*. Hessian ground, applied nets cut away in part to expose cotton cloth beneath. Knots worked in thin and thick wools and cotton embroidery threads.

Bullion knots

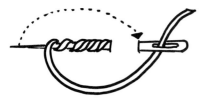

Sample worked in varying wools.

Bullion knots worked to give
impression of lilac tree blossom.
(Detail of *Dream Cottage* by
Eirian Short.)

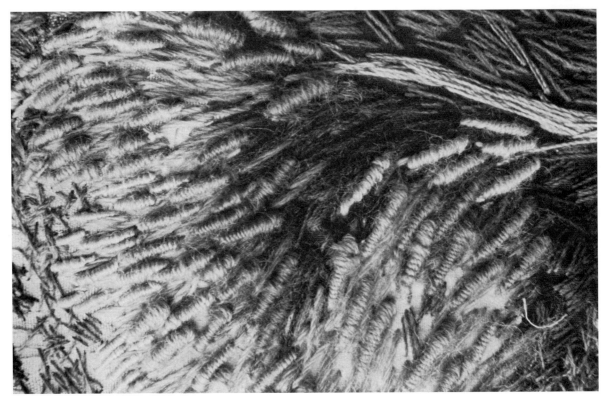

Seeding

Seeding: work running stitch in all directions fairly closely together.

Right
Sampler showing the stitch worked in perlita (thick and shiny), candlewick, wools, shiny cotton threads.

Below
Detail from a panel by Audrey Walker. Thick knitting yarns, perlita (shiny, twisted thread) and strips of chiffon.

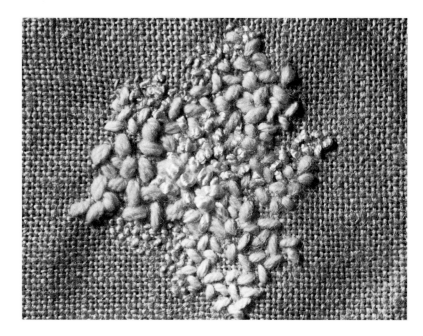

Straight stitches

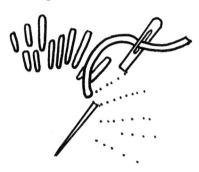

Right
Two examples showing blocks of
straight stitches worked in space
and close together to give tonal
differences.

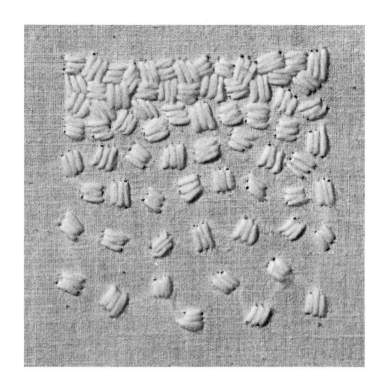

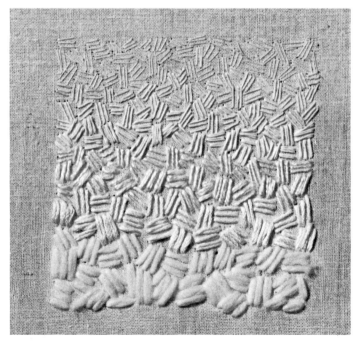

Opposite
Detail from *White Tree*. Knitting
wool and rayon straight stitches
worked beneath the tree to give a
quieter but interesting area to
contrast with the blossom detail.

Buttonhole filling
—open

Button hole filling stitch—open.
Work a line of buttonhole
stitches first so that you have a
basic stitch to loop into. Work
the stitch in reverse when
working back from right to left.

Below
Sample shows a variety of thick
and thin threads deliberately
worked with uneven spacing
contrasting heavily worked 'lacy'
areas with holes. Some stitches
worked on top of others.

76

Buttonhole filling
–knotted

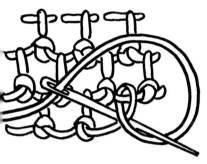

Buttonhole filling stitch—knotted. Work on line of straight stitches in the first instance to enable you to work into the stitch. Reverse the stitch on each return journey (from right to left).

Above
The stitch worked with regular spacing and tension in a cotton yarn.

Below
Buttonhole filling—knotted. Experiments with shiny, matt, thick and thin threads worked with irregular spacing.

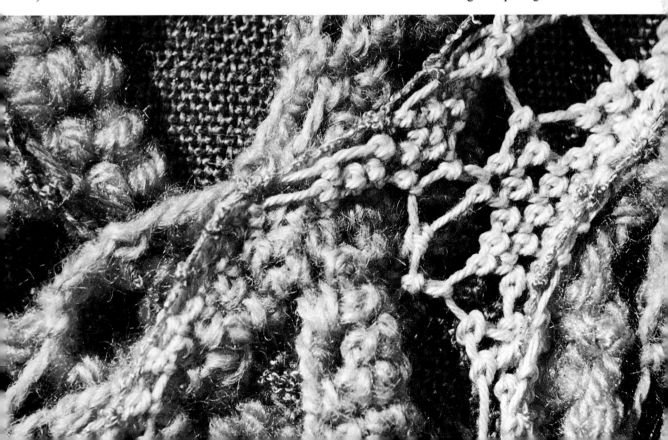

Questions to ask

If at any stage of its development your panel suddenly seems to bewilder you or something seems wrong—stop and systematically ask yourself the following questions:

1   Are all the shapes too regular—equal in area—not related one to another?

2   Are the spaces between the shapes
        —pleasing to look at?
        —being developed?
        —overworked so that the design has lost its structure?

3   Is the panel too 'busy' and therefore confusing? (Remember to have some plainer areas to allow the more detailed ones to 'breathe'.)

4   Are you using too many stitches?

5   Is the textured work in keeping with the design? (If small unrelated areas of rich texture are dotted all over the panel the design could lose its unity.)

6   Has the colour scheme gone astray?
Are there too many colours?
(Equal areas of colour can be confusing and boring. Emphasize one colour and have smaller amounts of 'helping' colour.)

7   Is your interpretation too literal? (The design may need to have fewer details—to be a simpler statement.)

8   Is there a tonal problem? (Look at the panel through half-closed eyes. Is there any shape which

is too dark or too light and 'jumps' out of the picture?)

9 Does the composition seem to be changing from your original intentions? (This is not always a bad thing.)

10 Make sure your focal point is still important. (A strong line, a very thick area of stitching, very shiny, light, dark or brightly coloured areas could be misplaced, attracting the eye away from the main point of interest.)

Stretching and Mounting

If the embroidery has been worked in the hand or only moderately stretched on a frame, the work will need to be improved by stretching (*see below*). Ironing is not suitable as the stitchery will be flattened.

Embroidery stretched over damp paper on a board and pinned tautly all round with drawing pins. Try and ensure you keep the grain of the fabric straight.

Back view of an embroidery stretched over hardboard. Having folded the edges of the fabric over the board, lace with a strong (nylon) thread from the centre to the outer corners. Fold the corners neatly and oversew in place.

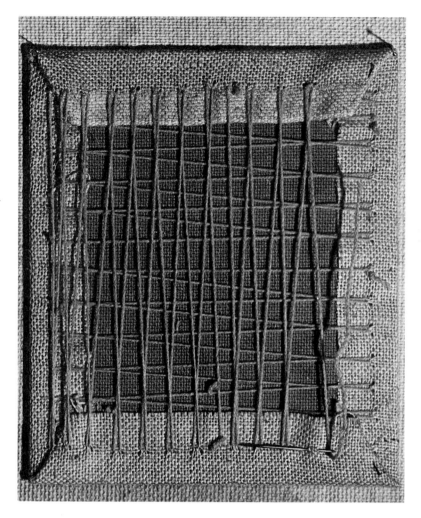

If the panel has been tautly framed during the working, stretching with damp paper is not necessary; the panel can be removed from the working frame and laced over hardboard (*see above*).

Some embroiderers do not use hardboard and insert the working frame, with the embroidery tightly stretched, directly into a picture frame. This is particularly helpful when dealing with large panels, as hardboard would have to be battened to prevent warping and thus making the work heavy to handle.

Panels need not be glazed: spray them with a fabric protector such as Scotchgard. (Do ensure you read the maker's instructions.)

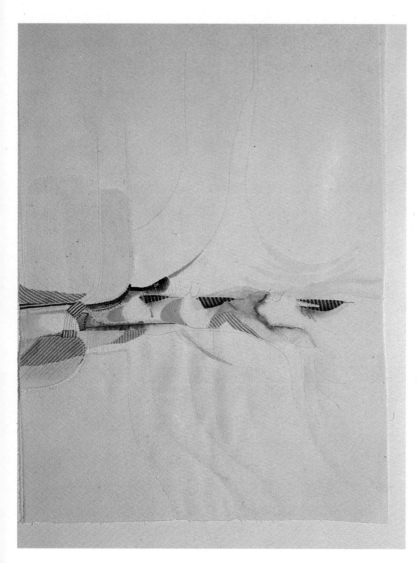

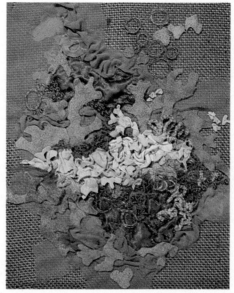

Experimental embroidery
inspired by drawings of lichen
(Jan Beaney). Hessian ground,
applied leathers, net, quilted
rayons; couched, knotted and
looped wools and chenille
threads.

Awakening I by Audrey
Brockbank. Applied sections of
cotton shirts, sheeting stained
with coloured inks. Machine
stitchery and small areas of
straight stitches.

Autumn Landscape by Jan
Beaney. Basic shapes painted
on hessian ground with Dylon
dye. Shot fabrics and nets were
applied. Straight stitches, knots
and cretan stitch were worked
mainly in perle, coton à broder
and soft embroidery threads.

Autumn Landscape—detail.

Embroidery: Different Approaches

The methods and approaches suggested in the earlier sections of this book have been those I have found most helpful for my students. Their purpose is to help the beginner master the basic techniques which will provide the essential groundwork for his or her own individual interpretations.

But of course there is no one and only way: each designer has his or her own individual approach. In this concluding section I have attempted (for, as with other art forms, creative embroidery is largely an intuitive process) to define my own approach and have asked five other professional designers to describe theirs.

For some years now, in my own work, I have been inspired by landscape and in particular the colour, tonal and atmospheric effects that changing weather, light and the seasons have on these subjects.

I usually make a number of sketches of a particular subject varying the viewpoints. Generally, I select a section from a sketch simplifying or emphasizing the shapes into a pleasing composition. At the same time, I try and retain the original concept. This might involve intense colour or textural qualities, certain patterns, spaces or views beyond or 'catching' a fleeting change of light or atmosphere.

Most of my panels include some appliqué with a limited number of stitches worked in a variety of matt and shining threads when applicable.

Painted design taken from a pencil sketch of a section of the water garden at Cliveden in Autumn. (Paint, fibre-tip pen and coloured crayons.)

Cut-paper shapes of the basic shapes were assembled into a simple composition.

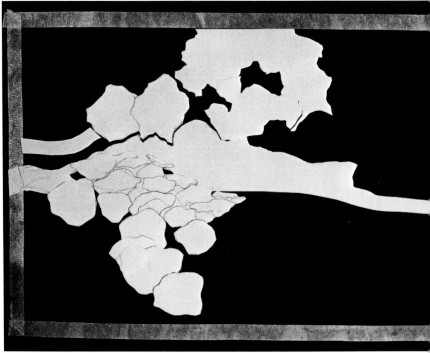

The design was traced, squared
up and drawn on a larger sheet
of paper.

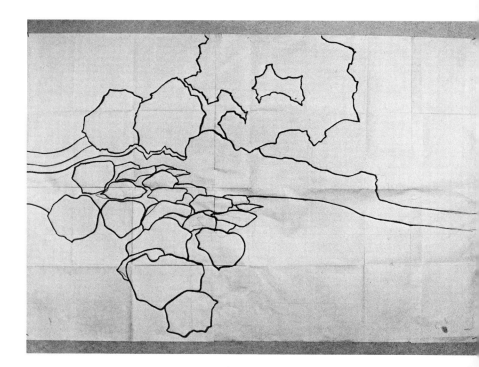

The completed embroidery :
Autumn Landscape (see colour
plates facing page 81). The basic
shapes were painted on the fabric
with Dylon. Net was applied and
straight stitches, couching, cretan
stitch and french knots were
used.

Audrey Tucker

River Between Trees I (pen drawing)

'This is a drawing made in a simplified way, by drawing the outside edges of the trees and trunks. With this approach to drawing you eliminate all the confusing detail—the result being a collection of shapes.

'As this is a flat pattern of shapes, I have treated the embroidery in a flat way. The stitches are straight which give no surface texture, but a variety of threads give some textural interest by being shiny or matt.'

Poppies and Nasturtiums (See colour plate facing page 49)

'The original drawing for this embroidery is in oil pastels and coloured charcoal pencil. I used colours to match exactly those on the plants, as it was the colour that attracted me most, even though the subject has a certain pattern quality.

'On the embroidery I used the thread like a drawing media and sewed as if I was drawing, using matt cotton thread. The finished embroidery looks to me far more exciting as the thread gives a textural quality which is not possible with crayon.'

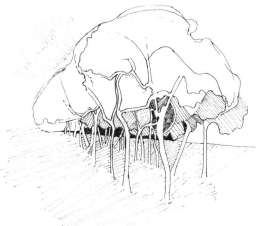

River between trees I (pen drawing).

84

River between trees II (pencil drawing).

River between trees III (embroidered panel).

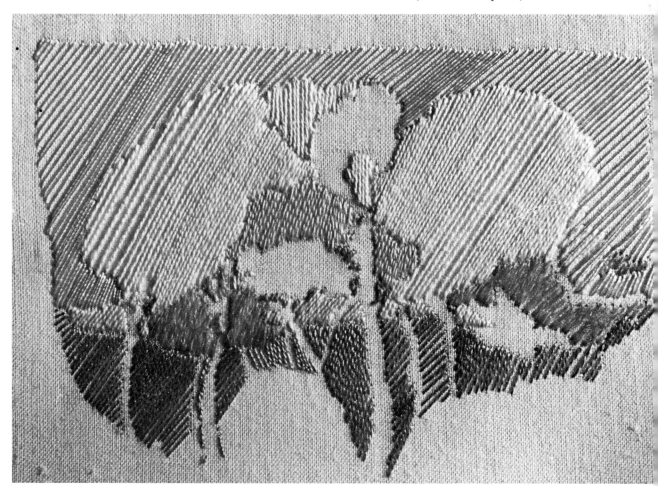

Audrey Brockbank

1

I generally start work with the fabric. I have an instinctive preference for white, e.g. shirt or sheet. I enjoy the inexhaustible and subtle changes of light on a white surface and the tactile quality of natural washed and worn fibres.

2

Various stimuli contribute to the content of the work; for example, in the plates in this book, the stimuli included:

(*a*) Fragments of old fabric, pressed under glass with frayed edges, in the Victoria and Albert Museum.

(*b*) The cloth itself, where it touched the body, its natural creases and folds, the shapes of the shadows.

(*c*) The graphic quality of old garment labels. C. E. Muybridge's sequential photographs of *Woman rising from bed*, particularly the movement of the sheets.

3

Composition.

The composition is initiated by the framework of the fabric and developed rather in the way of a painting, by the application of colour, dyes and stains, striped areas, machined lines, applied patches and threads, etc.

4

Finally, it is important that the composition is not static, although by necessity it must be a caught moment. I try for a sense of space and freedom, even in the smallest piece of work.

Sketch for the panel *Awakening I*. (See colour plate facing page 80.)

86

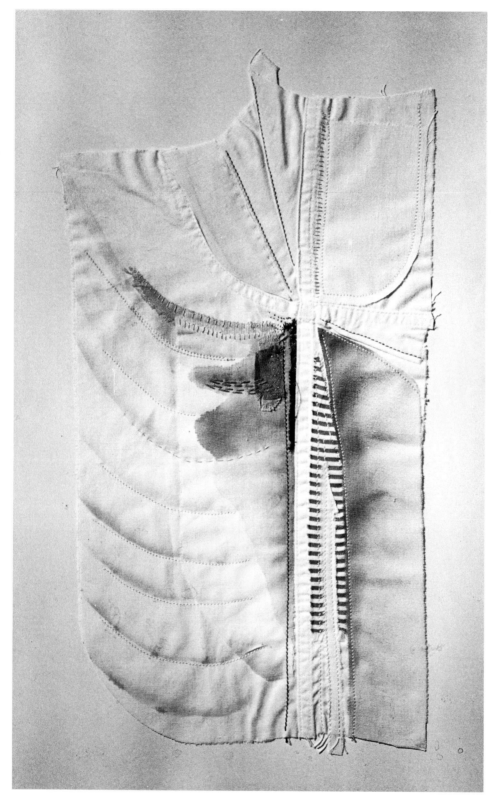

Shirt fragment—Audrey Brockbank.

Dream Cottage by Eirian Short.

Eirian Short

'The work shown incorporates two ideas which have interested me for some time.

> 1 *Symbolism:* after several years of researching into and working with symbols of life and death, I turned to symbols of happiness.

> 2 *Popular Art:* I have always been intensely interested in the kind of things that appeal to people who have *not* had an art-school or an aesthetic training, nor have an acknowledged standard of "good taste".

'Both these elements fuse in depictions of crinoline ladies in lavender gardens, bluebirds flying over the rainbow and cottages with roses round the door. The pictorial element is often reinforced with a sentimental motto. For reference I turned to our local flea market where I collected fire-screens, silver-paper crinoline ladies behind black-painted glass, wall plaques and biscuit tins. These formed the basis of a batch of work, two pieces of which are shown here.'

To a Friend's House by Eirian Short. Stitches include french and bullion knots, detached chain stitch, stem and straight stitches.

88

Richard Box

'The scene represents the moment when Paris presents the golden apple to Aphrodite for being the most beautiful of all the goddesses.

'The inspiration for the design partly comes from Attic black and red vase paintings. The economy and understatement of the formal elements evoke the drama and narrative rather than depict it. Therefore, devices like the symmetrical displacement of the figures, the simple profile views, broad open areas to balance the more complex details, a simple and high-pitched colour scheme and unobtrusive embroidery stitching are all examples of how a quiet tranquility is attempted.

'Several colour drawings were made. The figures themselves derive also from Attic vases in part as well as from other varying sources, all of which are combined or translated to make a new form. The total composition of the interrelated characters is equally if not more important than individual figures and forms.

'The final solution was enlarged on paper to the size of the intended collage and used as a template.

'Colours and tones of the materials were chosen to suit the final drawing. They were cut out precisely and applied to a large piece of material which also forms part of the picture. All material was attached by a satin stitch by a swing-machine. Some hand stitching was finally added for relevant details.'

Above
Design for *The Judgment of Paris*.

Below
The Judgment of Paris—panel.

Darned face—Audrey Walker.

Audrey Walker

Sketch-Head . . . 1976

'This small head (approximately 30×27 cm or $12 \times 10\frac{1}{2}$ in.) is one of a series of experimental sketches in which an attempt was made to build up an image directly by means of very simple textile processes. In this case a coarsely woven cotton fabric was used as a base and on it a few main structural lines were drawn in tailor's chalk. Thereafter the areas were gradually built up by darning into the fabric with yarns of varied thickness and tone. Some areas were given further textural contrast by withdrawing threads and distorting the woven fabric.'

General Statement—but related to Summer Window *I* (*see colour plates facing page 33*)

'The everyday experience of looking through curtained windows at different times of day, in changing light and onto a shifting pattern outside the window, has led me to a series of embroideries of which this is the first.

'About two years before starting any of these embroideries I had made a painting and several drawings on this "window" theme. My embroideries at this time were more about the garden itself, but in 1977 the two ideas came together.

'Scraps of lace, fabrics dyed or painted and fragments of partly completed embroideries were the raw materials to start the work. These scraps were assembled together, simple zig-zag machine stitching made up broad areas of colour and the textural quality was gradually built up and unified by direct hand-stitching of a very simple nature. I work as directly and spontaneously as possible with the fabrics and thread-building up, cutting out, re-working and re-assembling in an attempt to make a coherent whole—to translate the idea into an image which grows through the textile medium.

'This particular window idea had been evolving for about two years and in the beginning some detailed factual studies had been made. However, in working the actual embroidery no further preliminary drawings were used. The first "marks" were made by cutting, tearing, pinning, arranging and re-arranging. I like to keep the work "fluid" for as long as possible so that radical alterations can be made at almost any stage. Quite often this entails cutting up a partly completed piece and re-assembling it on a new base fabric.

'Each piece, and each stage of that piece must be an adventure or it is not worth doing.'

Julia Caprara

Sea Drift by Julia Caprara. Embroidered panel based on the movement of seaweed over rocks. Wrapped straight stitches, french knots, couched threads and wooden beads.

'I work with threads, fabrics and stitchery rather than paint or sculpt as these materials somehow develop a denser, richer surface closer to the qualities of light, colour and form of the visual world around us. I aim at creating my own kind of order from the visual chaos around us—to work parallel with nature rather than to illustrate natural form.'

Books to read

Looking and drawing

Jan Beaney: *Buildings: in picture, collage and design* (Pelham Books)
Jan Beaney: *Landscapes: in picture, collage and design* (Pelham Books)
Jan Beaney: *Textures and Surface Patterns* (Pelham Books)
Kenneth Jameson: *You Can Draw* (Studio Vista)
Maurice de Sausmarez: *Basic Design: The Dynamics of Visual Form* (Studio Vista)

Stitches and Techniques

Anne Butler: *Simple Stitches* (Batsford)
Thérèse de Dillmont: *Encyclopedia of Needlework* (Mulhouse, France D.M.C.)
Nik Krevitsky: *Stitchery: Art and Craft* (Van Nostrand Reinhold)
Mary Thomas: *Mary Thomas's Dictionary of Stitches* (Hodder & Stoughton)

Machine Embroidery

Jennifer Gray: *Machine Embroidery: Technique and Design* (Batsford)
Christine Risley: *Machine Embroidery* (Studio Vista)

General Design and Embroidery

Hannah Frew: *Three Dimensional Embroidery* (Van Nostrand Reinhold)
Valerie Harding: *Textures in Embroidery* (Batsford)
Constance Howard: *Inspiration for Embroidery* (Batsford)
Constance Howard: *Embroidery and Colour* (Batsford)
Mary Newland and Carol Walkin: *Printing and Embroidery* (Batsford)
Eirian Short: *Introducing Macramé* (Batsford)
Eirian Short: *Introducing Quilting* (Batsford)
Kathleen Whyte: *Design in Embroidery* (Batsford)

Magazines

Craft magazine published every two months by Crafts Advising Council, 28 Haymarket, London SW1Y 4SU
Embroidery magazine published quarterly for the Embroiderers' Guild by de Denne Ltd., 161 Kenton Road, Kenton, Harrow, Middlesex HA3 0EU

Transparencies, visual aids can be obtained from:

Focal Point Filmstrips Ltd., 251 Copnor Rd, Portsmouth PO3 5EE
The Embroiderers' Guild, 18 Bolton St, London

Suppliers

Needlewoman Shop,
146–148 Regent Street, London
W1R 6BA
(General embroidery materials—
threads, linens, etc.)

MacCullock and Wallis Ltd.,
25–26 Dering Street, London
W1R 0BH
(General embroidery materials)

Nottingham Handicraft Co.
(School Suppliers),
Melton Road,
West Bridgford,
Nottingham NG2 6HD
(General embroidery materials)

Mace and Nairn,
89 Crane Street,
Salisbury,
Wiltshire SP1 2PY.
(General embroidery materials)

de Denne Ltd.,
159/161 Kenton Road,
Kenton, Harrow,
Middlesex HA3 0EU
(General embroidery materials)

Cotswold Craft Centre
5 Whitehall,
Stroud,
Glos. GL5 1HA.
(General embroidery/threads,
weaving yarns, beads)

Needlework Notions,
1 Cambrian Way,
Paston, Peterborough
Cambs.
(Fancy yarns, hessian, beads, etc)

John P. Milner,
67 Queen Street,
Hitchin,
Herts.
(leather off-cuts)

Dicksons and Co. (Dungannon)
Ltd.,
Linen Manufacturers,
Dungannon, Co. Tyrone,
Northern Ireland.
(Linen/theatrical scrim)

The Weavers Shop,
Wilton Royal Carpet Factory,
King Street,
Wilton, Nr. Salisbury,
Wilts. SP2 0AY
(Thrums, long ends of unsorted
yarns)

B. Brown (Holborn) Ltd.,
Warriner House,
32/33 Grenville Street,
London EC1N 8TD
(Hessian, felt, muslin)

Maharani Boutique,
10 Quadrant Arcade,
80–82 Regent Street,
London W.1.
(Shisha glass)

Ells and Farrier Ltd.,
5 Princes Street,
London W1R 8PH
(Beads, sequins)